INSPIRATION FOR THE
ENTREPRENEUR

BOSSY

JAZMINE ROCHELLE

Paper Trail focuses on bringing holistic inspiration to the literary world. All stories are not meant to depict, portray, or represent a particular person or place. Religious notations mentioned are not to defame or negate any other religion.

"All scriptures mentioned herein are taken from the Holy Bible New International Version, unless otherwise stated."

ISBN: 978-0692865446
Cover Design: Jazmine Rochelle
Layout Design: Write On Promotions

Dedication

This book is dedicated to every believer opposed to settling for status-quo—B.O.S.S. May your every *Boss* move be a production of purpose and promise. May you forever maximize your BOSS potential as you strive to thrive!

Acknowledgments

To my mother, Joy, thank you for being an example of poise and perseverance. To my spiritual parents, Apostle Travis, and Pastor Stephanie Jennings, thank you for prophesying and pushing me to produce this book. Without you three standing as my influential support system, and without your prayers, this book would just be a dream of mine—not my reality.

Day by Day

Day by Day

BOSSY

Inspiration for the Entrepreneur

"For we are God's handiwork, created in Christ Jesus to do good works, which God prepared in advance for us to do." (Ephesians 2:10)

DAY #1
PURPOSE TO PRODUCE

You are on your journey to becoming and embracing the 'boss' that God has fated you to be. Understand and believe that prior to your father meeting your mother—before you were conceived and formed in your mother's womb, God created and purposed you to produce something in the earth. Your production was strategically planned. God ever-so-carefully handcrafted you and placed within you every skill you would need to produce the businesses, the organizations, and the innovations that He destined you to establish on Earth.

All this may seem exciting, intriguing, and even a little inspiring; however, make a mental note that while you have been created on purpose with a purpose, God's ways are not our finite human ways, nor are His thoughts as miniscule as our thoughts. God's actions may not align with our expectations. His delivery may rarely coincide with our will. This statement I know to be true in my personal life.

Journal Entry #1

"She has a pretty easy life. She was probably raised with a silver spoon in her mouth." Most would think that upon assessing my age, college degree, profession in education, and status as a successful entrepreneur. Yeah right though— silver spoon! That is not my reality. Never has it been the golden ticket put to my mouth. Quite simply, life provoked me to take over the world– and so, in stride, with a cute pair of heels, I do!

Through the most unlikely vessels, God gave me the gift of life. My biological parents were perverted and confused drug abusers at the time that I was conceived. As unfortunate as it is, and like so many others, I was a child born and rejected. At three-weeks-old I was given up for adoption. There is no sad story here though. I know God's ways are different from mine and so are His thoughts. The mere fact that my thoughts are penned for publication legitimizes God's purpose for my life and His intentionality for yours.

From one 'boss' to another, embark on life's journey. Be intentional in embracing and maximizing your 'boss' potential. As you do this, rejoice in knowing that you have been strategically created with a purpose, on purpose, which is to produce.

"Blessed is the one who perseveres under trial because, having stood the test, that person will receive the crown of life that the Lord has promised to those who love him." (James 1:12)

DAY #2
POWER TO PERSERVERE

Knowledge is power, but it is the application of knowledge that is key to being a successful 'boss'. Knowing that you have purpose alone is not enough to produce anything. You will need power to persevere through this journey. Life will throw you some curveballs and you will experience highs and lows. Yes, inevitably, you will have good days, and you will most definitely have bad days. However, this must not prevent you from producing what you were purposed for.

Is it always easy? Heck no! Will you always "feel" like it? Uhm, of, course not! You have to push pass those emotions, rest in assurance, and stand firm on what you know the end result will be—regardless of the lemons life throws at you. The God you serve is big! He is the God who just so happens to know how to make lemonade. This is a cup I've become quite acquainted with drinking.

Journal Entry #2

God sweetened my "lemon-like" entry into this world, by blessing me with the best adoptive parents a child could ever pray for. Through their lives, I gained an understanding of what perseverance really looks like. I grew up watching my dad battle against diabetes. His bout with the disease led to the amputation of one of his legs and a few of his toes, yet he persevered daily. Every day he pushed through and chose not to allow his physical inabilities to affect his inner abilities to be an active father to me and a loving husband to my mom.

In true form, my mother gracefully stood by his side without mumbling or complaining. She would go to work each day, come home to take care of the house and my dad, and stood poised beside my him—honoring him as the king of our castle. You see, my power to overcome life's obstacles was not inspired by friends, or even celebrities. My power to persevere was evoked from the tremendous perseverance that my parents lived out right before my eyes. They did it despite the unexpectedly hard situations that were thrown at them.

Most that hear this story view it as sad or disheartening; but for me, it stands as a pivotal reflection of great faith, character, and strength. I am the woman that I am today because of their power to persevere.

From one 'boss' to another, let today be a day of reflection and rejoicing. Be glad in the fact that the situation you are currently experiencing, others have also been in, and have quit—or even died in it. You however, keep pushing to gain the win! Those of you fellow bosses that are still in the stage of persevering—you too can rejoice! The fact that you are still present shows that you still have victory in view. Your win is right around the corner.

"My grace is sufficient for you, for my power is made perfect in weakness." (2 Corinthians 12:9)

DAY #3
GRACE TO TRANSITION

Boss, you are progressing on your journey! I am certain that the walk thus far has been quite interesting. If you're having a similar experience to what I had when I first started, then I am sure you are admiring the amazingness of God. Today may very well be an ordinary day with nothing significant taking place. However, it is today that your sense of awareness will transcend to another level.

Within the last couple of days, you have come to find that there is purpose for you in life. This level of understanding is provoking you to live life outside of the emotions of fear, give up, or even laziness. The dots in your life are connecting. The pinnacle of revelation in this day should be you seeing how God has consistently assisted you every time life has taken you in another direction—

knowingly or unknowingly. This is the grace of God.

It must be understood that you did not get to 'boss' status, and will never truly be 'bossy' on your own. When you are working the long hours to produce work for your demanding clientele, while working a nine-to-five job for someone else because you have to fund the business that you run; and along with those things you are enrolled in school because you understand that skills without credentials is like a car without an engine–useless! The grace of God is that which keeps you from passing out from exhaustion. It is His grace that continues to drive you when you feel like your dream is more than you can handle.

Know that we never really give life permission to knock us upside the head. Life tends to be a rude and uninvited guest. It barges in unannounced and does what it wants to do with no consideration of how it will make us feel. Trust me! I know grace. It became a true companion during the biggest transition of my life.

Journal Entry #3

My mind is filled with the not so distant memory of April 26, 2000. My role model, comforter, and the captain of my fan squad is gone. I called him daddy. I can never forget when my mom woke me up with the look of indefinite despair. She told me that my dad had gone to Heaven. I was only nine years old, and somehow, in that moment I felt it was my place to be strong. The emotion of uncertainty, I chose to mask in fear. I knew not what the future held for my mom and me. Our lot had been casted, and my dad had transitioned from labor to reward. It was only fitting that we too moved on—right?

I mean life had just came in and sat her rump in our living space. No questions. No heads up. No compassion. It is surreal to me how my mom and I had to now reacclimate to one another. We had to become familiar with each other's new ways due to the transition. We both had taken on new roles too. My mom was no longer wife, but was widowed-single-mom. Me, the "daddy's girl," was now a fatherless child—or so it seemed.

Though the obstacle of my dad's passing and everything that came with it was overwhelming, we overcame. We conquered mountains together, and through it all we did it with grace. God graced us to transition through the ordeal of losing the head of our home. Just the same, as we were graced, you too have you been given a measure of grace to triumph in any transition you encounter.

From one 'boss' to another, I encourage you to boss up today! Reflect on the tragedies, trials, and tests that you've been through within the past few days or even years. After doing so, celebrate! Rejoice in the fact that circumstances that others could not get over or get through, you did—gracefully.

*"Therefore, my beloved brethren, be ye steadfast,
unmovable, always abounding in the work of the Lord,
forasmuch as ye know that your labor is not in vain in the
Lord."* (1Corinthians 15:58)

DAY #4
PUSH TO ABOUND

Oh, the push that is coming, is about to be real. When an object is pushed, it is said to be thrusted forward with forceful momentum coming from behind. As a 'boss', you are the object that will constantly be thrusted forward with forceful momentum. Life, people, and at times, even you yourself will demand you to push to greater levels of accomplishment and acquisition.

Think about it; when is the last time you did something that you were afraid to do? What is it that you dream of having, seeing, being, or doing that you talk yourself out of? Now consider why it is that you do that. It is necessary for you to defy complacency, self-doubt, and fear by taking on new feats. Not to be a voice of cliché here, but seriously, the only thing that beats a failure is a try.

The reason for this is because even if you try and fail, you are far ahead of those who have never tried. Isn't that amazing! If the truth be told, you know of a lot of people that have yet to try anything that they've thought of. You don't have to look for it, it's very evident in their lack of passion, productivity, and progression

Your 'boss' status demands you to be great. As my pastor, Dr. Travis C. Jennings eloquently stated, "greatness comes when you commit to challenging yourself every day to be better than yesterday. As you challenge yourself, keep in mind that you are your competition if no one else is. Step out of your comfort zone. I dare you! Why? Because as my pastor has said, "comfort is the trap door to poverty and discomfort is the doorway to development."

You'd be surprised how much you can accomplish in life and how much of a 'boss' you really are, once you grasp that there is more to life than mundane everyday comfort zones. The only way to get more out of life is when you are push to abound. Yes, I know pursuing new things tend to be a bit frightening and mostly uncomfortable, but living stuck by a severe case of the "what ifs" is not living at all. You are empowered to succeed, and what you think is unattainable can be done—allowing God to be your power source of course.

Journal Entry #4

Coming out of prayer one morning, I was in awe of how God had just blown my mind! He orchestrated my steps even the more. My memory took me back to my fifth-grade days when I desired to try out for cheerleading.

The "chubby girl" is what they called me in elementary school. Let's just say that my baby fat had overstayed its welcome. I was smart with a great personality—if I do say so myself, but that did not matter to my peers. They teased me about my weight constantly. Needless to say, this made me insecure about my weight. I started to think poorly about myself, just as girls that are in that situation commonly do.

Cheering was something I knew that I could do. My weight, self-doubt, and the whispers of others about my dream to be a cheerleader had to be pushed aside so that I could even tryout for the squad—and I did. I pushed every one of those emotions aside in an effort to abound towards my dream. It was a successful attempt because I made the squad. I cheered all the way up to my senior year.

I wish I could take all the credit for conquering that goal, but I can't. Within me I felt a push to try. I felt a need to go for it. That was God letting me know that it wasn't impossible for the "chubby girl," for lack of a better term, to make the cheerleading squad. It was worth it too, because I ended up becoming the captain of my squad in high school.

Do not allow past attempts to hinder you from trying again. I didn't! I did no let the words of naysayers or my insecurities stop me from setting and accomplishing my goals. It was a push well needed. It multiplied my esteem, faith, and influence.

From one 'boss' to another, celebrate the fact that your past did not paralyze you. Take a good look at where you are; your past has pushed you to abound. There are some of you who may still be in the push. Rest assured that you can and will come through this because you are not alone in the push! You have an unseen force fighting for your win!

"You intended to harm me, but God intended it for good to accomplish what is now being done, the saving of many lives." (Genesis 50:20 NIV)

DAY #5
EMPOWERED TO INFLUENCE

Every situation you've gone through, mountain you've climbed, or battle you fought is not for you alone, nor is it by happenstance. Your life is designed to influence the lives of others, whether it be negatively or positively. You, my fellow 'boss' have been empowered to influence. You see, influence is defined as the capacity to affect the character, development, or behavior of someone or something. As a 'boss', you must work to ensure that your influence does a good work for those that glean from you.

We accomplish this goal by being intentional and careful of how we carry ourselves, along with how we handle others. Influence comes whether you mean for it to or not. You never know whose source of influence you have become.

People are always watching. The impact that you could have on someone else's character, development, and behavior is not a right, but a privilege to be honored, so don't abuse it.

Journal Entry #5

Cheerleading! I am so glad that I did not let past situations stop me from taking that step to abound. Back then, I was so much more confident than I'd ever been. I had self-confidence and was evolving into a better version of me. My mind is still blown by all that had taken place in my life. I could not believe that I was in a selected role of leadership. I remember the girl that was not confident to even tryout for the cheerleading squad, but did, and became the captain.

I began to influence those that were a part of the team. They were looking to me for advice, direction, or as a sounding board for their aspirations. The feeling of being able to help others just by being myself sparked a deeper drive in me. Who knew that a push to abound would provoke me to step further outside my norm? Without trying, I was leading in multiple facets. In my school, church, and even among my friends, my boldness to lead influenced others to do, want, and believe for better.

From one 'boss' to another, note to yourself that there is a lot for you to hold your head up about. What the enemy thought would stop you, has empowered you to gain influence to become another person's source of encouragement. Your yes to bossing is the start to someone else's yes to believe!

"Be confident in this very thing, that he, which hath begun a good work in you, will perform is until the day of Jesus Christ." (Philippians 1:6 KJV)

DAY #6
POWER TO PERFORM

You are being enabled to accomplish the purpose in which God created you to. Whether it be evident or a mystery to you, know that purpose is being fulfilled and your promise is bound to perform.

Performance calls for one to carry out, accomplish, or fulfill a thing. You are a 'boss', and I have no doubt that you will perform in premium status; it's just what bosses do! You have spent just about a week getting in touch with the fact that you have been purposed to produce. You have power to persevere and grace to transition. Getting this far is your push to abound that is going to empower your influence. The best is yet to come for you!

Journal Entry #6

A journey that begun with a desire to share my story with the world was now becoming a story, rewritten by God, right before my eyes. While praying one Sunday morning before church I repetitively heard the voice of God say to me "power to perform."

It was a multiple service kinda' Sunday. Pastor Stephanie preached about Multiplicity. That message sounded like my journal entry from the other day—push to abound. In the second service, the Apostle Jennings touched on performance—sounded like power to perform.

Through all that God shared with me that day, I distinctly remember Him saying that He is giving me the power to perform! Despite my past hurts and failures, shortcomings and seeds of doubt, God says to me that He is giving me the ability to carry out, accomplish, and fulfill every promise and purpose that He has on my life. Please do not be salty. In no way am I boasting in myself. All that is happening for me, God has done, and the same fate is in store for you.

From one 'boss' to another, do not get caught up in reflecting today. Choose however, to look ahead because you are moving forward. Today, promise, progress, and purpose is your portion. The stage is set and it is your time to perform.

"In the same way, faith by itself, if it is not accompanied by action, is dead." (James 2:17)

DAY #7
PREPARE TO EXCEL

When bossing, it is imperative for you to know that what you have to offer is in high demand. Believing this is not you being cocky. Even if you are just starting your 'bossy' journey, so what! You must believe that you've got the goods, and while you are believing that, you must be ready for those goods to be asked for in high volumes. With this in mind, do not short change yourself by being ill-prepared. Bosses must live with a mindset that constantly has them preparing to excel.

How often have you prayed for a thing, but have not properly prepared to receive it? Did you pray and ask God for more clients, yet you have not even designed a business card? Brief sidebar here...you do know that there are websites where you can design and print a business card for $10—

right? So, there is no excuse. Okay, I'm now backing away from my soapbox and returning to my original point. When you pray for things, the next step is to prepare for it. Bosses must always go there, before they get there!

We serve a God that is able to do exceeding, abundantly, above all we could ask or think. You have the power to perform, but do not let that energy within you go to waste by not properly preparing yourself to excel. Being 'bossy' is all about going to another level. You must pay the cost to be the boss—put the right policies, procedures, and products in place. This way, when God blesses you with the demand, you will be able to properly supply the demand. Do you know that when you do not prepare for what you've prayed for, it is comparative to a lack or inexistence of faith? To pray for a thing, and not work to prepare for that in which was prayed for is a lack of faith, just as today's scripture reflects.

Journal Entry #7

I'm reminded of my prayers to God, asking Him to enlarge my territory, and to bless my endeavors and the gifts He's given me. Simply put, I prayed to be positioned to excel. As I recall it, to excel means to surpass, be exceptionally good or proficient in something. I was given the idea to design a shirt called B3 (Beauty, Brains, Believer) and to start the "good girls" movement. I had no idea that these ideas would be one for the books—literally! I knew it was divinely inspired. God gave it to me; so why was I not prepared?

This rhetorical question rattled my mind. Did I not pray and ask the Lord to bless it? Clearly my faith nor my expectations were at the level that God needed them to be for His blessing to be received on my endeavor. There was so much that should have been done and could have been done to supply the demand of the product I was offering.

From one 'boss' to another, do not set yourself up for failure by being ill-prepared. If you are believing for something, position yourself for the outcome—expect it to be great. Today, get to work preparing for what you've been expecting. Rejoice in the fact that you are about to excel, and there will be no issue because you will have prepared!

"What good will it be for someone to gain the whole world, yet forfeit their soul?" (Matthew 16:26)

DAY #8
CALLED TO SURRENDER

Bosses aren't employees, we don't quit! Every day you won't feel like it. In fact, today you might not even want to be reading this book, or you probably don't want to do something that you should be doing to invest in your business or your brand. I need you to go ahead and die to that. Remember that to excel, you must prepare. Today, your point of preparation will be a state of surrender. True surrender will demand you to relinquish your control to an entity other than yourself. Although this may be tough, it is necessary! You see, being 'bossy' has very little to do with having power, but everything to do with how that power is attained and maintained. You are building an empire, and preparing your legacy. How are you accomplishing that?

What are you giving up to ensure that success is your portion? Bossing requires you to surrender your lazy ways to your 'bossy' days. Your state of surrender must be constant—especially to God. What will you have truly gained if you become this mega mogul with no peace, wealth, or genuine happiness? Constant surrender helps to ensure that your success is healthy and sustained on Earth.

Journal Entry #8

Complacency with old victories in God will always do you in. You must forever seek to reach higher heights and deeper depths. As a 'boss' and a believer, how dare I forget that I must stay in a forever state of surrender to God.

I specifically recall that He worked this out for me, yet, my pride has me expecting Him to do it the same way, at the same time, this time around. Yes, He is the God that is the same yesterday, today, and forevermore, but his execution in manifesting things does change.

Who am I to boss Him around—is He not God? He is the supreme boss; yet, I feel the need to offer my assistance. I find that I am oftentimes reminding myself of this fact. God is so good, and does so much for me that it has become easy to get comfortable with the way He blesses. However, I must be committed to faith and submit to His plans, His way.

From one 'boss' to another, I admonish you to surrender your will and your wants to God. I know it will seem that you are giving up a lot, but why not give up a lot to gain everything?

"For I know the plans I have for you, declares the Lord, plans to prosper you and not to harm you, plans to give you hope and a future." (Jeremiah 29:11)

DAY #9
PREPARE TO PROCESS

Evolution is inevitable—here we grow again! So, again, I say, it costs to be the boss. One of the most constant checks you will cash in your journey to becoming 'bossy' is process.

I hear you! "Oh God, not process again". 'Boss', process is not a bad thing. It is a term that has become negatively connoted. It is a term of dread, especially among Christians. Why is that, when process simply means to change (a thing) from one form into another by preparing, handling, or treating it in a special way? Are you a boss that is afraid of change? I would hope not, but if you are, let's shift your perception of what process is.

With God, process is synonymous to elevation. We are transcended from one place to another through process. He does not do it to aggravate us, or annoy us. He is simply readying us for our future. Process helps one to be bold, be brave, and ultimately be 'bossy'.

Journal Entry #9

My process was not easy, but day by day I saw how it was worth it. I saw that I am the apple of God's eyes. He was and is my father and no good thing will He hold back from me. It is only fitting that He would prepare me for the future He already planned for me. No use in getting ready when I get there. I have to be ready now. I was often reminded that I was fearfully and wonderfully made by God, so I should be certain that He would handle me with special care through this process.

Process has been around since the beginning of time. People like Abraham, Job, and Esther are all examples of people that have undergone process. They went through a lot of pressuring, and unforeseen events, but at the end of it all, they were all elevated. As a good Father,

God provides the best child support. Abraham ended up being the father of faith. Job, lost everything, only to be rewarded with double of all things that he had lost. Esther, well this orphan girl who lost her parents and had a very humble living experience, became the queen of an entire kingdom. Progress comes with process. I made the conscious decision to not give up in process.

From one 'boss' to another, take a deep breath today and push. The only way out of the process is to go through the process. No one is exempted from process—especially not bosses. You are either in process, coming out of process, or preparing to go back in. 'Boss' up and celebrate, because you are one step closer to your promise.

"My dear brothers and sisters, take note to this: Everyone should be quick to listen, slow to speak and slow to become angry." (James 1:19)

DAY #10
STOP TO LISTEN

Are you a 'boss' that hears but does not listen? Hearing takes effort, but listening requires intentionality. There are times on this journey to becoming 'bossy', that you will get stuck. It will feel as if you are at a fork in the road with no direction. Being stuck will more often than naught, make you swell with frustration. Remember though, none of this is being done to harm you, but to make you better than yesterday.

How often do you hear without listening? If you are stuck and have been stuck for some time now it is possible that you need to listen more. Listening is the best way to sense your next move. Do your best not to get caught up and flustered on swiftly moving through the process that you miss what God is saying to you through it all. Shift your focus from going through your process to growing through your process. When you shift your focus, and listen you will avoid prolonging the process. Because God is the creator of time, time is set to obey His command; so, God has all the time in the world—literally, but you don't! Maximize your time in process and listen.

Journal Entry #10

Recalling a conversation I had with a friend of mine, it baffled me the numerous ways that God had told me the same thing. It was almost as if He was in Heaven saying, "I'm not gonna' stop saying it, until you get it! There were so many ways that He attempted to speak, yet I'd been so busy trying to get through the moment, that His voice seemed to be fainting by the days. While I knew that the voice of God was projected through music, people, situations, and His word—otherwise known as the Bible, I must not have been listening. How many more times will he relay this same message to me? I guess when I stopped talking and started listening, I would hear Him speak.

From one 'boss' to another, listen. It's not the end of the world if you haven't been, but you now need to get in the habit of doing so. Remember, the only way out is through. You have a better chance of getting through your process if you choose to listen to what God is saying today. Your choice to listen today, could be the turning point of your tomorrow. After all, God's words are worth listening to. His words give life to dead situations, strategies for your success, and leads you to your promise.

"Beloved, I wish above all things that you may prosper and be in divine health, even as your soul prospers."
(3John 1:2 KJV)

DAY #11
PLAN TO PROSPER

Failing to plan is planning to fail. How many times have you heard this before? Real bosses know this to be true. You must live by a plan. Without a plan, you are like a deer in headlights, just moments away from becoming road kill. It is time that you become acquainted with the plan to prosper.

It is His heart's desire that you flourish as your 'boss' potential evolves. His plans for you are holistic. It's His will that you flourish spiritually, mentally, emotionally, and financially. Take what you learned from yesterday, and apply it here. Listen to the voice of God. All the ideas and strategies you need to make it to 'boss' status already lie within you. Shut out the noise of life and embrace and embody God's predestined plan for you.

Journal Entry #11

Many days I felt like I was here, there, and everywhere. However, it comes with the territory. Although often said, I truly found that to whom much is given, much is yet required. The funny thing is, had you asked me, I would have imagined that entrepreneurship would be in my view. However, as a boss I came to accept that: [1]God is the originator of the plan and has the right to change it at any given moment. [2]When God gives the green light to make a move, the plan must move forward in execution. [3]God's plan will only bring prosperity if I am consistent in working it.

From one 'boss' to another, become aware of the plan that is set in place. Today, choose to be happy in the knowledge that God wants you to prosper, as do I. You have a backer that not only gives you the plan, but has equipped you with all that is necessary to prosper that plan as you carry it out.

"Trust in the Lord with all your heart and lean not on your own understanding."

(Proverbs 3:5)

DAY #12
FAITH TO FOLLOW

If your vision does not frighten you, it is not big enough! Hopefully, you are not arrogant to think that the dreams you have can happen by your ability alone. If you've ever muttered "this plan is too big for me," guess what? You are absolutely correct! God gives us plans bigger than ourselves so that we can be a testament to others that we serve a big God who can make big things happen, but adherence to the plan is key. We have to make sure that our faith to follow the plan is just as big as the God who created the plan.

Journal Entry #12

After having a great day, I began to freak out. I couldn't believe my birthday was almost here and my entrepreneurial journey was about to start. I was so nervous and had no real idea as to why. I could not for the life of me figure out how everything that I had to do was going to get done in preparation for my big day.

I felt overwhelmed and inadequate. I had no time to clean up the mess that I was becoming from the stress I was carrying. God knew that, so He got me right together before I fell apart. In a still small voice I heard, "I gave the vision, so I will give the provision. Just stick to the plan. Do what I said told you." These words were like music to my ears. My mind was finally at ease.

From one 'boss' to another, great promises are headed your way and they are big. It is tough and oftentimes lonely in this process. It may very well be a struggle; but today, whatever you do, and no matter what life throws at you—show that you trust God by faithfully following His plan.

"I will lead the blind by ways they have not known, along unfamiliar paths I will guide them; I will turn the darkness into light before them and make the rough places smooth. These are the things I will do; I will not forsake them."

(Isaiah 42:16)

DAY #13
PREPARE TO SHIFT

While the quick fix to being 'bossy' is nonexistent and the elevator to success is broken, there are stairs! I get that with the day and age that we're living in, everyone wants it quick, fast, and now. However, when bossing you must be willing to go against what you thought you knew, and tap into the unfamiliar. This my friend is called shift.

Shifting often makes you uneasy and uncomfortable. You will not always be sure of what is coming next, or in which direction you should be headed. Quite frankly the only surety you'll have when a shift is taking place, is that something unexpected is about to happen. This part of your journey can and will be one of the most discomforting stages that you encounter. However, you can sustain in the shift by staying in constant communication with God. He will give you divine direction with every fork in the road that comes.

Journal Entry #13

I knew that I was going through transition, but I was not quite prepared for the shift that came with it. I was in a different place, with different people, and ideas around me had changed significantly. God was taking me from where I was to where I was supposed to be. However, never did God allow me to get comfortable. It never failed, when I felt like I had finally gotten the hang of things where I was, here comes shift, altering, and changing my direction. I was finally a believer that shift happens!

From one 'boss' to another, take the day to assess your next strategy. The truth is that you have already shifted, so now, you are just seeking direction for the next turn. Rejoice in the fact that you are being directed and positioned by God into greatness.

DAY #14
CALLED TO CONQUER

The climb to the top is lonely. Being a 'boss' naturally comes with its share of challenges. One of the greatest trials you will encounter is attempting to possess the goals that are set for you while deciphering the motives of those around you. This is a taxing and oftentimes discouraging set of events, but you have what it takes to overcome this.

Not everyone can endure the climb, and not everyone will want to do what it takes to ensure that you keep climbing. There is not one 'boss' that you will meet that will tell you that they have not encountered this scenario. It comes with the territory. Just as they did, you too must own this obstacle and conquer it. Know that to conquer means that you will possess and overcome it.

You will only get to where you are destined to be, and will only produce the purpose that God has placed on your life, comparable to who you allow to handle you as you scale your mountain of influence.

Journal Entry#14

In my feelings, I could not figure out why what I was looking at looked nothing like what God said. I needed a break of some sort because this seemed to be too much for me to handle. Just thinking of that day made me laugh because my inner tantrum was checked by friends who had no problems setting me straight.

They shut down the emotional soundtrack that my feelings had on repeat in my head. They echoed to me what God had shared about my purpose promise, and potential. I appreciated them for not just being there to push me when I was strong, but they lifted me up when I was weak.

I am now able to reflect over my life and remember all the things that I have conquered thus far. Seriously though, I was a chubby girl with low self-esteem, and now, I am a woman that thinks highly of herself. I conquered my fears with faith.

The sicknesses that I faced, I overcame them with healing. The grief and sorrow that I once had, is now exceeding joy. Goodness! How could I be so blind as to not see that?

From one 'boss' to another, take today to celebrate those around you who have not allowed you to give up. It could be family, friends, or coworkers. Whomever it is, know that they and God have your back. You will conquer all.

"I press on toward the goal to win the prize for which God has called me heavenward in Christ Jesus."
(Philippians 3:14)

DAY #15
POWER TO PRESS

Water breaks are few, far, and in between for bosses. The climb is going to require you to press. You must press pass giving up, pass giving out, and pass giving in. Just like bosses throughout the world, you are going to have to 'boss' up. Remember that you are more than a conqueror. Your ability to get it done is not what's in question. What we do need to determine here is your 'want' in getting it done.

Again, life is not going to just let you win and accomplish your goals. There are fires that are going to come up and issues that will arise within your business or even your personal life that could derail your attention from the ultimate goal. This is where you must 'boss' up and press pass the obstacles. Stop putting out little fires and extinguish the fire source. Stop majoring in the minor—get your priorities together and major in the major. These are the kind of methods that will help prevent you from feeling overwhelmed on the journey.

Journal Entry #15

It is so true what they say, "time waits for no one." After sobering up from that tangent of emotions that I allowed myself to fall into, I was making up for the lost time. I got so consumed by everything that I saw happening, or 'not' happening around me, that I just stopped moving. How could I allow life to continue to move without me? There was so much work that I had to put in to even get to this point, and I just up and let it go—why—because I was expecting a few things to happen and they didn't? How immature was that!

The price that I paid to be better than yesterday, no one would ever truly understand, but as long as I kept pressing, I was well on my way to gaining my goal. I knew it was not all about me achieving my dreams, but fulfilling my God-given destiny. Therefore, I had to and still have to press.

From one 'boss' to another, choose today to look beyond what you see and take in what lies ahead of you. This is a good day to get a press in your spirit. You have what it takes to be greater than the game called life. You are more than a conqueror with the power to press through to the finish.

"The thief comes only to steal and kill and destroy; I have come that they may have life, and have it to the full."
(John 10:10)

DAY #16
DARE TO DREAM

Steve Harvey coined the phrase, "the dream is free, but the hustle is sold separately." This is true—know it! The 'boss' will at times be overwhelmed with the process of becoming 'bossy'. Quite honestly, while bossing you will feel like quitting because what you envisioned is not what you see. This is the stage of the journey where most bosses start walking by sight and not by faith.

Be careful here, because what you see can cause you to pause your purpose which will eventually hinder your dreams. So, it's imperative that you walk by faith and not by sight. You must stand firm on what you know, and believe that that which you know, God has purposed it, and you will not fail in producing it.

Making 'boss' moves will not be the hardest thing you do, but it will also not be the easiest. Life will come and boy does it come strong. Although things may be going well in your life, the little 'not-so-well' things will be magnified in your sight to frustrate you and make you doubt what you know you should be doing. Life is a weapon, often used against you to delay your forward movement. Notice that I did not say 'stop' because the truth is, there is nothing that can stop the will of God from manifesting through your life. You are oh, so close to attaining that which you've prayed for and all that you've been diligently preparing for. Why let life stop you? Dare to dream and if you're going to do it, do it big!

Journal Entry #16

I was ready to let everything go and just give up. I sat there bargaining with God, knowing that I had to shake that off.

I literally had to say to myself "Jazmine, you've got to shut up…get up…boss up!" I quickly found out that the best way to persevere is to dream again. So what? I thought it was supposed to happen and it had not. Who said that it wasn't going to? Life had done it's best to hurt me. However, I chose to hurt life back by simply being great. You are more than a conqueror, remember? Do not allow the start of your journey to stop you from reaching the end of it. The best revenge to life's attempt to hinder your progress is dreaming and attaining your purpose. Dreaming motivates you to live your best life—the abundant life—the boss life.

From one 'boss' to another, take your dreams off pause, and kick em' up a notch! Once you start dreaming again, do not waste your time on small exploits. Today you have the greenlight to dream big! Let your dreams be so big that they require more than just you to accomplish it.

"Again, truly I tell you that if two of you on earth agree about anything they ask for, it will be done for them by my Father in heaven." (Matthew 18:19)

DAY #17
CONFIDENCE TO CONNECT

The air of confidence is necessary when being 'bossy'. You cannot be a person that just looks the part, but is not yet 'the' part. Whether we choose to admit it or not, we are people that have a fear of rejection. Some of us deal with it on more severe levels than others, but at some point, in time, we have all talked ourselves out of connecting with someone so that we are not rejected. We do this because we are afraid of allowing our fears, failures, and flaws to be noticed by anyone beside ourselves.

True bosses do not hide. You have no reason to, because when you hide, you hinder the evolution of upcoming bosses that suffer from similar issues. You don't want to be a stumbling block, do you? I would hope not. So, get some confidence about yourself. My fellow 'boss', you need to know that you are uniquely, necessarily, different and in high demand. The world needs what you have to offer.

Yes, it is quite possible that onlookers will view you as cocky or even arrogant, but there is a difference in those from that of confidence. A lack of confidence will have you down playing the knowledge of your expertise in an effort to make those less knowledgeable comfortable in their incompetence. Lacking confidence will have you complacently hiding in the shadows of others, because you are afraid to step out on your own.

This is not you—nor is it who you have been purposed to be. This is a false identity, designed to limit your progress and stunt your momentum. You are greater than that—you are bold, brave—you are 'bossy'! Your next level depends on it, and so does your opportunities. It can be a bit much, but more can be accomplished when you do it with help.

Journal Entry #17

I've dealt with rejection since birth. My spiel was targeted towards looking the part. Most have no clue, but this 'boss' was shy. I did not like speaking in front of large crowds. I didn't even like venturing out to meet new people. When in a room full of unfamiliar people, I felt invisible; at, least I hoped to be. The irony of it all, right?

These types of scenarios made and sometimes still make me increasingly nervous. I often avoided a number of business relationships, clients, and lifetime opportunities due to my lack of confidence. This is the old me though. I am glad to say there has been some change in this department; no thanks to me of course, but all thanks to God. I realized that He had been putting me in those situations. Confidence was being demanded of me.

My constant exposure to these scenarios made me 'boss' up. I gained a new-found freedom in embracing all of me, even the not so together parts. Since then, I have been working my confidence so that I can connect with those that

God has raised up to use their power, ability, and influence to help produce my purpose.

From one 'boss' to another, know that there is power in numbers. Learn from my experiences and do not allow yourself to miss opportunities today. Think of that person that you've been avoiding having that conversation with—initiate communicate now. Do not allow your idiosyncrasies to deprive you of connecting with others. You have no idea who you can help or who can help you because of it.

"—From everyone who has been given much, much will be demanded; and from the one who has been entrusted with much, much more will be asked."

(Luke 12:48)

DAY #18
PREPARE FOR PROMOTION

Purpose is not a facet that stands on its own, for with it comes promotion. Promotion alludes to elevation, which is upward movement. This is what you want. This is the outcome of being 'bossy'. It would be a sad thing to be known by such a title, yet have no progress behind the title in which you've embraced,

You are not going to wake up in the morning and stumble into promotion. It is not a case of happenstance. In order for promotion to be yours, you must prepare for it. This is another case of going there, before you go there. You know that 'faith-thing' we talked about earlier—you're going to need that here. When God sees that you have unwavering, bulldog tenacity fueling your faith, promotion will kiss your purpose. But, before you go getting all excited, how have you prepared for promotion?

You want to be ready for promotion and all that comes along with it. Yes, you will be noticed more, and you may very well gain more monetarily. However, the higher you go is the more responsibility that will be required of you to stay there.

Journal Entry #18

Thinking of the transitions that took place over the years, I reminisced on the lows and the highs in both states of circumstances. I was happy that I never gave up on God or the promises that He had for me at the time. I did however come close.

I prayed for years for my territory to be enlarged, there were even higher heights that I desired to be taken to—but I had to ask myself, "what have you done, Jazmine, to prepare for such ways to be made? You do know that God is a gentleman, right? He will never force Himself on you, so you must give Him your permission and your participation for Him to do that which you desire to be done."

From one 'boss' to another, take the time today to honestly answer the question, "If God gave you everything that you were praying for right this minute, would you be able to accept it and maintain it? It is the way to determine if you are really ready for the promotion God has for you. If your answer to this question is no, that is okay. Start preparing yourself now. Do the necessary research, put plans in place with dates attached to them. Doors are opening for you, but to walk in them, you must have prepared completely.

"I will make you a great nation, and I will bless you; I will make your name great, and you will be a blessing."
(Genesis 12:2)

Day #19
READY FOR REVOLUTION

There is a revolution coming and you are a part of it. Do you believe it? It's been over two weeks now, so you should be settling in comfortably in your new-found 'bossy' regimen. Your presence is going to cause a stir. You are going to revolutionize your area of expertise. Just as the inception of Wi-Fi revolutionized how people communicated, attained information, and even did their jobs.

When Wi-Fi hit the scene, the internet was never the same. When you hit the scene, that is how it's going to be. The key point here, is never being the same—changing the game. Like yesterday, there is preparation that will need to be in place. However, the preparation this time will be on God. He is going to prepare you by bestowing His favor on you.

God's favor is multifaceted; not only does it benefit you, but it blesses those connected to you. This is why confidence to connect is so important; there is someone in need of the favor of God, and their portion of it will come through you.

Journal Entry #19

Being humbled in knowing that others will be blessed because of my yes to endure and duke out this journey. I was inspired to be the change (revolution) that I desired to see. Where God was taking me, He was also setting it up that things would never be the same for me, those connected to me, and for those that would encounter me.

I guess this is why I am uniquely, necessarily different. Life as I knew it was about to change, and I couldn't fathom why I was the one to walk it out, but the journey has been showing to be one well worth it. I was being prepared to revolutionize my mountain of influence.

From one 'boss' to another, be prepared not to blend in, but to stand out. As a revolutionary 'boss', you will not be noticed, you will be known. Today, I encourage you to attempt to fathom not just having enough, but having more than enough, and living a life well suited for the revolutionist you are destined to become—to the point that those around you will be able to eat too.

"But to each one of us grace has been given as Christ apportioned it." (Ephesians 4:7)

DAY #20
GRACE TO LIVE

Experience is the greatest teacher, and as a 'boss' you will come to know that this statement is not a cliché. Experience has a way of highlighting just how much of a thorn your short comings are, along with the impact they possess. Let's just say that experience has a profound way of showing bosses worldwide, just how much we need God.

A true sign of being 'bossy' is understanding that you are not perfect although those around you will tend to view you as such. To be viewed as perfect is not a bad thing, but it does come with a level of responsibility. As a 'boss' you must remind yourself every day that you too are entitled to make mistakes. You are human, and you too have weak points, bad days, and areas that need improvement.

Now don't you go getting excited here. This is not a free pass for you to go out there and make cavalier mistakes. Remember, you are a 'boss', and the standard is held higher for you than the average person. I mean seriously, are you not trying to establish, expand, and expose your empire throughout the world? Certainly, you are going to get weak in the process of doing all of that!

Remember a few days ago, you learned that with God all things are possible. Well, living beyond the weakness is no exception. To be honest, I truly believe that we are all embedded with a thorn of weakness, just so that we remember that we are finite and with limitations, and are very much in need of God, who is the infinite one, having no limitations. God is able and willing to help you conqueror any weakness, but You have to allow Him to help you. If not, experience will gladly come in and put you in a position where you have to. How embarrassing would that be to look over the one that says, let me help, and then have no other choice but to go back to Him when you find that you don't have what it takes to help yourself.

Journal Entry #20

Hi! My name is Jazmine Rochelle, and I was and still am my worst critic. I am so hard on myself when I 'feel' that I've fallen short of a goal or a projected expectation. I usually would retreat into hiding, but I didn't even have the time to do that. I was certain that others handled the weakness of failure differently, so my way of coping wasn't too bad—was it?

I can just imagine how amused God must have been in that moment. He does not strike me as a God that responds to threats, tantrums, or tears. My way of coping wasn't a way to survive, so there was no true retreat in sight. I often asked myself how was I to do this? How was I supposed to get up and 'boss' again when my situations had knocked me down to a weakened state? The only thing I could consider at that point was to humble myself and remember that God's grace is sufficient in my times of weakness.

From one 'boss' to another, know that God's grace is strong enough for you to rise above weakness. Today, when that thorn in your side sticks you deeply—say ouch, take a deep breath, and then exhale with gladness. By the time you let that breath go, you would have been endowed with God's grace to live through the pain and execute your purpose with accuracy and precision.

"—He wakens me morning by morning, wakens my ear to listen like one being instructed. The Sovereign Lord has opened my ears; I have not been rebellious, I have not turned away." (Isaiah 50:4-5)

DAY #21
DESPERATE TO HEAR

Yesterday a brief mention was made regarding how others view you. You learned that oftentimes others look at you and think you are perfect. We've also established that to be false. You see, the cold hard facts will reflect that the people around you, whether acquaintance, friend, foe, family, or self—they will have something to say about what you are doing, and what direction you should take to get there. This is a trap, that you must look out for daily. It is not to say that all that is said will be negative, but it is to say that it will be noisy; and where noise is—who can hear clearly?

You may be wondering, why is it so important for a 'boss' to be able to hear? To put it quite simple—the more people you encounter, the more voices you will hear, and the more voices you hear, the more likely you are to encounter noise. Thank goodness you have an office. It is the one place you can shut the door and control the direct noise that you're exposed to daily. Your office is your secret place, whether it be in your home or a distant location.

The office in this instance is the place where you have solitude, peace, and most importantly silence. This is your secret place and the voice of God is your secret weapon. No one can hear what you hear, or take the ideas, directions, and strategies that He gives to you. You are going to need and must rely on the voice of God in order to live your best life— the 'boss' life. When the noise of everyone else is tuned out, you can hear the voice of God clearly. So, get you some noise canceling headphones, still away in your office, and just hear Him.

Journal Entry #21

I was baffled at the fact that it had been three weeks, an entire twenty-one days of me accepting the challenge to be 'bossy'. Who knew that I had such drive—certainly not I. I'm sure

God did though. It is because of me listening to His voice that I got to that point in life. I was in a constant state of desperation to hear His voice. It's like I couldn't and shouldn't make a move without first hearing from Him.

I'm amused because I remember when it was a struggle. I often fought to silence the voices of everyone, including my own. I had to lay down my thoughts and opinions to hear what God had to say to me. It was the only way that I could gain wisdom, direction, and understanding—which are three factors every 'boss' needs to be successful.

When I listened, I was always in awe of just how many great exploits and blessings He had in store for me. I was so glad to be in a place where I could hear the voice of God. Transitional times are endless in the line of work I'm in, so I need the voice of God to ring in my ear.

From one 'boss' to another, take today to tune out or turn off the noise around you. This won't be the easiest task on your list. Remember, life is always waiting to throw distraction your way. Your purpose desperately depends on you mastering the ability to simply stop and listen to the voice that will lead you to your destiny. Choose to listen to no other voice than His.

"The light of the body is the eye: if therefore thine eye be single, thy whole body shall be full of light."
(Matthew 6:22)

DAY #22
DETERMINED TO FOCUS

Earlier in this journey I cautioned you to life and how she uses tactics called distractions to deter you from being in 'boss' mode. Well, ponder this thought. What if life took a back seat today and you became the culprit guilty of plaguing your journey with distractions? Bossing requires you to be honest with yourself. So, go ahead and swallow that pride—I'll wait!

There will come a point in the process where you take your eyes off the prize and start looking elsewhere. Life will have nothing to do with it; this one will be all on you. The reason this will come about will be for one or more reasons. You may get bored with the task at hand. You may get so prideful, thinking that you've got it all under control because things are going well, so you take a quick glance in another direction. You may very well shift your attention just to rebel against the process, because you are tired and ready to be processed out.

No good will come from this. You must have tunnel vision when bossing. You must intensify your 'block' game and perfect your methods to 'curve' any person or anything that could divide your attention. You must, as today's scripture reads, have single vision.

When someone sees double or more than that, they oftentimes have difficulty differentiating between the real and the fake. They see two of everything and must focus harder to determine what they are really seeing. Which sounds to me like a lot of time and energy wasted.

Journal Entry #22

Promotion was coming and I had been found guilty of being distracted. I wish there was someone, or something that I could blame it on, but the charges were on me; I distracted myself.

It was so crazy how I allowed my attention to be shifted. I had gone from bossing to being captivated by other people and situations that had absolutely nothing to do with my promise, process, or purpose. So much time was wasted with this. Mentally, I had to kick everyone out, and undo that which should have never been done in the first place. Talk about time wasted.

I invited people and situations in to rent space in my process, and was overworking my purpose to fix the mess that could delay my promise. I couldn't believe that I was my own distraction this time around—ain't nobody got time for that!

From one 'boss' to another, stay focused. Your productivity depends on it. To lose your focus at this stage of the journey will put you in a state of playing catch up. Do not allow your vison to become scattered, because you will end up spending the day jumping through hoops—and last time I checked, you were a 'boss' not a circus animal.

"But remember the Lord your God, for it is he who gives you the ability to produce wealth——."
(Deuteronomy 8:18)

DAY #23
EXPECT TO SUCCEED

Do you know that with God, you've got this? Do you know that the works of your hand will not just be a figment of your imagination, but a fact of your success? You have come this far by faith, perseverance, endurance, and grace. None of which came from you just being so awesome and wonderful. Each of those attributes came as a gift from God. He knows what it takes for you to produce purpose here on Earth. It is He who enables you to be the 'boss' that you are.

There is so much that I am certain that you've encountered while on this journey. What's ironic is that you have not even hit the tip of the iceberg of all the greatness God has in store for you. Can you believe that this is just the prelude to your beginning?

Your belief in your success is pivotal to the manifestation of your success. You have to do more than wanting and believing in your success, you have to have to expect success. You do not want to be known as the 'boss' that "just" has visions, and "just" have dreams. No! This type of action is considered nonchalant.

You want to take the God given visions and dreams, and produce them for the world. For you to not produce that which God gives you is a sheer reflection of your faith—or lack thereof. I get it though, you're afraid, as you very well should be. However, you are not in this process alone. God is with you every step of the way to ensure that the purpose He put in you is produced. He is the one that gives you the ability to 'boss'. Know that your success will not come separate from Him.

Journal Entry #23

Things had not been gumdrops and gummy bears. The ride had most certainly extended its share of prickly pears and sour patch kids. Despite it all, it was a pleasure. The maturity that took place in me was astonishing. I could honestly say that I had more clarity concerning my life.

It is through maturity that I could voice that numerous chances and opportunities I missed because of the nonchalant attitude I had. Needless to say, my lack of faith, and preparation had cost me both time and money. I have no one to blame but myself. I dare not throw a tantrum with God, because last time I checked, my arms are were too short to box with Him.

Naturally so, I got caught up in my feelings and emotions. That was a result of me forgetting that when God gives vision, He makes provision. My only job in the process was to prepare, participate, and produce. God's portion was to do the hard part, He was to provide, protect, and promote.

From one 'boss' to another, don't let my plight be your fight. Remember that God begun the work, and He will complete it if you stay active in the process. Today, live with the expectation to succeed beyond your wildest dreams—and if you've stopped dreaming, do your destiny a favor—dream again!

"He says, be still and know that I am God— "
(Psalms 46:10)

DAY #24
JUST BE STILL

You know, it's easy to get overly excited and move out of place when we think about the exciting things God is doing in our lives! I mean, after all the run-ins that life has dealt us, it would almost be a shame not to celebrate the goodness of God when we can clearly see it.

Having zeal and enthusiasm is great. As a 'boss' you do not want to be guilty of not having either of those things when you are pondering the future God gave you. However, you do want to be leery of allowing those attributes to put you in a position where you move ahead of God. Yes, you too must wait. You must be patient in waiting, while holding on to the fact that God will grace you to endure the weight as you wait. You my 'bossy' friend, must learn to stand still and allow God to be just that—God.

In your position of "ready", you must also note that you have to "get set". When you consider track athletes, they first have to get ready, then get set, before they are released to go. They don't just take their marks and then start running. My God, could you imagine how much of a mess the Olympics would be? Could you imagine the chaos and commotion that would take place at the meets? I am amused just picturing it.

This is why being still is so important. It allows you to show that you are ready to take off, as well as it gives you time to assess the course that is ahead of you before you start running towards the finish.

Journal Entry #24

Thinking about what a catalytic moment I was about to experience, I thought "this will be one for the books"—literally. I truly believed that life for me was about to change. I was ecstatic about it, but the excitement of it all, nearly cost me the execution.

I took matters into my own hands and provoked promise to occur for me. How disappointing that outcome was. In fact, the outcome of it was a mess of shambles. God gave me insight to my future and I came out of that thing full speed ahead. I planned, organized, strategized, and went on making things happen, with no clue as to the why behind what I was doing. This was just another way of putting myself in my own way. As I considered the mess that I'd made, I imagined God sitting there looking at me as if to say—girl, I'm gonna' need you don't go have several seats!

From one 'boss' to another, when God gives you a glimpse of what future has in store for you, take a note from me and wait on Him to release you to move forward. The end-result of standing still will be so much greater than the outcome of uncontrolled zeal.

"When he had finished speaking, he said to Simon, launch out into the deep, and let down your nets for a draught."
(Luke 5:4 KJV)

DAY #25
PREPARE TO LAUNCH

Launch! That word is one that every 'boss' will utter one or more times within their journey. It is a common term because bosses are always launching or relaunching an idea, or product. There are web launches, brand launches, product launches, and the oh so popular, business launch. No matter how you slice it, as long as you are called 'bossy', you will be launching vision to the masses.

To do this successfully you will be required to thrust forcefully through your place of comfort, to your place of call. You must operate beyond your present potential, and start manifesting promise. Launching, will put a demand on you far beyond what you can imagine. It is only when you move from knowing your passion, to pursing said passion, that your concealed status will shift to a revealed status.

You are no longer in the "ready" "get set" part of the process, honey, you are in the "go" and all lights are green. This is a great place to be because you did not let the start stop you. Bossing requires you to stay in a positon of temporary discomfort, so that you can permanently develop and thrive. How many people do you know will endure discomfort for any length of time? Yet, unlike most, you are doing what's necessary to make the big catch.

Bosses are those filled with deep water potential. You are not afraid to do what is necessary to succeed. This is not to say that you are not or will not be afraid, or even slothful, but it is to say that you will do what is necessary to make it to a successful end. At the end of the day, this is what matters. Executing your deep-water potential to make the ultimate catch, will keep you bossing far beyond today. You bossed up, and now you are in position to make 'boss' moves that will positively affect the way you live life.

Journal Entry #25

It was my 25th Birthday and the day that I launched my business. That night had been titled *The Emancipation*. It was only fitting that I called it that, seeing that I was being set free from the person that life created. I would be walking into the person that I was destined to be.

I couldn't believe that I was minutes away from experiencing a day that would change my life forever. How exciting—right! I mean, I had been waiting for this moment all my life—well for most of my life. I could think of no other way to end the first quarter of the year.

From one 'boss' to another, choose today to be excited about your process and your progress. I am certain that you too will celebrate a major launch, relaunch, rebranding, or business deal sooner than you think. Know that the best is yet to come for you!

"Do nothing out of selfish ambition or vain conceit. Rather, in humility value others above yourselves, not looking to your own interest but each of you to the interests of the others." (Philippians 2:3-4)

DAY #26
REMEMBER THE PEOPLE

The gift of entrepreneurship is just that—a gift. If you think that the bright ideas, you have, came about solely from yourself, you are sadly mistaken. When God handcrafted you to do what it is that you do, He designed both your physical and spiritual makeup to encompass the entrepreneurial passion that burns within. In retrospect, you can say that the call chose you.

You were commissioned to do that in which you do. You did not beckon it. As stated before, entrepreneurship is a gift that God entrusts you with. You should cherish it and handle your craft with great care. The reason you must do these things is because that in which you do is connected to God's people. Your presence and purpose is linked to more than just yourself. As a 'boss' it is imperative to the success of your purpose, that you not forget the people.

The act of service runs conjunctively with the status of entrepreneurship. As you work to produce your products and services, remember that the most important factor within the production and the profit is the people. All these entities work together to establish the success you are striving for. There are bosses that give more attention to one entity than the other, but the end product never quite turns out as it should when this is done. People are your greatest assets in business. The client, the staff, the product, and the profit should all coincide to have a successful promise. They all work together for your good.

Now, I know that you may think that this is a rudimentary rule of thumbs for bossing—and you are right. However, as basic a principle as it may be, it is just as easily forgotten by bosses at times. The way to keep this at your forefront is to remember that people—otherwise referred to as clients, customers, consumers, and staff, are the ones who make it so that you can establish, maintain, and progress your 'boss' status. Without the people, you are not a 'boss', you are lost—a lost cause that is.

Journal Entry #26

Time flies when you are having fun and getting things done. I had made it to age twenty-five and launched my brand, but I couldn't celebrate my accomplishments without first thanking God for the people that He surrounded me with that helped me make it to that day.

Now, of course I knew that all those people were not supporters, but in some way or another, everyone played a role in the success of my emancipation! The reflection here is not too much about that, but more on the fact that I had to remember that the purpose God gave me has less to do with my life agenda and more to do with God's glory.

I'm not the president of the world or anything, but I did know that the mandate on my life influenced and impacted others. I had been entrusted with the responsibility of bringing visions pass the canvas of one's imagination and communicating it into a tangible presence for the free world to experience. I was not a one man show, and had people that continued to push me, help me, protect me, and pray for me as I did what I was called to do. I dare not forget them. I dare not mistreat them, because without them, there was no enterprise—there is no 'boss'.

From one 'boss' to another, while you create products, and receive profit, take today to appreciate the people assisting your purpose; knowing that it is all of that which makes your purpose move. By doing so, you will see that the way you do business will change and your measure of fulfillment will increase.

DAY #27
PERCEIVING THE FAILURE

Failure is not an option—but it is a common art in bossing that must be mastered. This subject may seem dauntingly dismal. However, I am here to tell you fret not! For bosses, failure is a vital and necessary contributor to your success story. Despite the negative connotations of its use, failure fuels your success. I can only imagine the look on your face at this moment. No one wants to fail, or bear the embarrassment that comes with it.

You see, failure is taboo in this so called 'boss' life. It is just like the unwelcomed virus we know to be a cold. As much as you take your vitamins, drink plenty of water, wash your hands, eat right, and exercise—you still end up catching a cold at some point throughout the year. To encounter failure is the same concept. You spend your days and nights working the vision, planning ahead, making all the 'boss' moves you know to make. Yet, and still something does not go as planned, and before you know it, the project or product you were working to put out, has come to a screeching, unwelcomed halt.

There are a number of books that have been written to highlight the fortune of entrepreneurship. However, the failures of entrepreneurship are scarcely mentioned within those pages. While I'd love to paint a pretty picture, and tell you that success will be your only portion, and that you won't encounter failure, I would be doing you a disservice and making myself out to be a liar.

What I will say though, is that failure works to your advantage. This is why it is necessary for success. Failure is an opportunity to perfect the imperfections of your business. To be a 'boss' is to understand that success is not an accident—you don't just fall into it. There is no silver spoon handed out that empowers you with all the know-hows to being successful. Everyone fails, falls short, or makes poor judgement calls at times, but it is what is done with the outcome of the matter that truly determines your bossiness.

Journal Entry #27

After spending countless hours and invested dollars into expanding a brand I had established, I now had nothing to show for it. This unfortunate event compromised my brand, and relationships had been affected. This was ludicrous and unacceptable.

I was super excited about this new product that I was to be launching. It was major and one that I had invested lots of upfront capital to produce; now things were not going as planned. To make a long story short, the product- could not be launched and the monies invested in the project had been lost. Can you say enraged and embarrassed? I was beyond both of those emotions, and upset at how it all panned out.

I felt Holy Spirit urging me to calm down, and surprisingly I chose to listen. You see, as much as I wanted to stay upset, I understood that what my pastor says is applicable in this moment. My feelings are understandable, and they are even explainable, but they are not justifiable. So, I had to accept that this had failed, not me. The perception of failure and failing had to be viewed differently from what I had become accustomed to.

It was crucial to my success that I learned that failure should be interpreted as forward steps to future, rather than backwards steps to the familiar. I must admit that I was not in the best of moods and did want my money back, but I had to say that because of this situation, I was set ablaze with a vigor, and gained a more discerning eye in moving forward. I chose not to revert to my normal ways of handling these types of situations. This too was working for my good; this too was making me better. Rather than fussing, I chose to go to work evaluating my focus, my fight, and ultimately the future of my business.

From one 'boss' to another, do your best today not to run from failure. When he knocks, open the door, and take advantage of his presence because he will most certainly be bearing gifts of knowledge. Let failure work for you. It will transform your mind and methods, which will cause you to grow.

"For we must all appear before the judgement seat of Christ, so that each of us may receive what is due us for the things done in the body, whether good or bad."
(2 Corinthians 5:10)

DAY #28
MANDATE TO MAINTAIN

The most important factor to being 'bossy' is taking care of yourself. While you are making 'boss' moves and producing purpose, you have to maintain your health. Remember that God wishes above all things that you prosper, be in divine health, even as your soul prospers. He is not a one-dimensional God, only concerned with you producing through the body, but not nurturing the body. It is your job to maintain the health of your body, by being intentional about your wellness.

Maintenance is important—and we're not thinking maintenance in the form of a mechanic, a maid, or dare I say, a sexual partner. The topic of maintenance that is on the table is that of your physical health. You must understand that while

God has given you purpose to produce, He does not want you to produce it at the risk of running yourself into the ground. This is why He gives us grace. Operating in the grace of God, is what will help you to keep your body up while making things happen.

Good health is important to achieving success. Do you not realize that you have been called to greatness? I implore you to make a quick note of it. You are held at a higher standard than others. Life is going to do her job and work to provide you with all the reasons why you cannot workout, rest, take a break, or go see a doctor. Being the 'boss' that you are, you must shut the excuses up and work towards a healthy you. Consider the last time you've been sick, sluggish, or tired. What did you do to take care of that issue? Did you chug, a large cup of coffee, or down a can of some overly caffeinated energy drink—did you go to the doctor for a physical, or take a full day to rest without calls and computers?

Be honest here, because the truth is what sets you free. The last thing you want is to have a purpose that prematurely goes to the grave with you because you did not adhere to the mandate for you to maintain your health. This is a perfect example of the scripture, to whom much is given, much is also required. This is the 'boss' life, and as stated at the start of this journey, you must pay the cost to be the 'boss'. Your success is only as healthy as the body that works to produce it. How can you meet the demands of your clientele if you are not physically or mentally well?

One truth that you should keep in mind is that you are a liability to your purpose if you do not ensure that you are physically able to produce it. I know that this is hard. Trust me, I struggle with this myself. I was once incapable of resting, and maintaining the proper health of my mind, body, and spirit. However, I now know the importance of maintaining my health, because I understand that when I stand before God, I will have to account for what was done—and in this case, not done, in this body.

Journal Entry #28

Sick again! I spent valuable time standing in line at the pharmacy—a place that I had become far too familiar with. In a span of three months, I'd gone to that pharmacy four times. This was not the life I wanted to get accustomed to living. Since launching my business, it seemed as if I had been physically ill more than ever. How could I really be surprised though? I had only been sleeping a total of twenty hours a week—and that was when it was slow.

My social media posts were laced with hash tags like 'team no sleep' and 'respect my grind', yet my health was failing; which in turn caused my production to fail. Now don't get me wrong, I understand the whole 'boss' mentality and the context of which these sayings are used. They are cute sayings, but the results they yielded were not so cute.

My business was only thriving at the level of my physical health. I had to go ahead and plan the staycation. The excuses, while they were good for everyone else, they were no longer acceptable for me. While I was at it I needed to join a gym, and find a workout partner. It was the only way to make sure that I did not end up back in this situation.

From one 'boss' to another, it may seem hard today, but please take the time out to reboot, rejuvenate, and revive your body. Your maintenance is viewed as stewardship, and you are responsible for the body which you're in. Some bosses may be able to take an extravagant trip, and there are others that can only do a staycation. Whatever you do, do it on your level. Today, go read a book, see your doctor, have dinner with friends—do something that allows you to unwind and maintain your body, mind, and soul. You're going to need all three in order to produce.

"Teach us to number our days, that we may gain a heart of wisdom." (Psalms 90:12)

DAY #29
REQUIRED TO PRIORITIZE

Failing to plan is certainly a planning to fail. This is not another one of those cliché quotes that makes one sound profound. 'Boss', this is a mantra that you must live by. You have learned how to make plans, but how do you manage the plans that you've made?

If you're anything remotely close to who I use to be, then you probably do not manage your plans well. You must number your days—literally. Get a planner that you keep on your person, and number your days. Unless you are a robot with the ability to compute the hours needed to complete tasks, you are going to have to learn to map out your plans so that you don't drop the ball.

Agendas and schedules are great tools to help you prioritize. Prioritizing is simply determining what's important. You must become a master of setting priorities. If you don't, you will be a 'boss' majoring in the minor and minoring in the major. Bosses naturally think that everything concerning their business is important—which is true. However, there are some aspects of business that are more urgent than others.

Do not waste time blowing out the candle when the entire house is on fire. When priorities are properly aligned, you become more productive. I'll be honest, one can function without prioritizing, but eventually, your functionality will fade. The place that you'll end up due to a lack of prioritizing is a state where wisdom will not be.

You do not have to be a 'boss' that learns the hard way. You can avoid stress and choose to strive by determining what's important, giving them a date and time on your agenda, and crossing them off as you get them done. Life is going to do its job to have you in a hectic state, and running all over the place. However, you have the authority to 'boss' up and kick life in the butt with a list of well thought out priorities.

Journal Entry #29

I sat drowning under a sea of invoices. The stress was definitely affecting my productivity, and the number of deadlines I'd missed—let's not even talk about it. I was not in a good place. My mind was cloudy and my creativity seemed to be nonexistent. For the life of me I could not understand why.

Was I not a 'boss', multi-tasker, C.E.O., a thinker for God's sake! None of those titles did anything for me. Whoever I was supposed to be, she had clearly taken the day off, and left me alone to sink in this ship.

Thank God for real friends though. Mine told me the truth that I do not even ask for and often did not want to hear. My oh so candid friend had the audacity to tell me that I needed to prioritize. I couldn't believe it. Being who I am, I retorted with a smart remark, that I had to swallow when I realized that they were right in their assessment. My priorities were out of order, and it had become evident, as my business donned the bruises that the internal bleeding of my scattered priorities produced.

From one 'boss' to another, reevaluate your task list. Determine what tasks are important for the business you are running. Once you've done that, make sure to write it down with deadlines attached to each of them. Goals without deadlines are wishes bound to be no more than thoughts.

"But I have this against you, that you have abandoned the love you first had." (Revelations 2:4)

DAY #30
STRIVE TO THRIVE

Congratulations! The business, organization, or product is up and running. You have managed to launch the business all while you worked your nine-to-five job, taking care of the kids, going to school, and probably a host of other things that I cannot think of.

Now, how do you feel? Is the passion that you had when you first began this journey to being 'bossy' still there? Has life sat on you so much so that you are burnt out with your own purpose? I have to ask because it is easy to get caught up in the routine of things, that before you know it, you've shifted from thriving to simply surviving.

Yes, the business is still in operation and you are probably even gaining clients and doing the work that you are used to doing—but what new exploit have you incorporated since the start of your venture? As with any entrepreneur, you will be working your business while managing your life outside of it. If you are not careful, you will find yourself guilty of producing your purpose without the love you had when you first began the journey.

Do not be dismayed; remember that God has your back, so all hope is not lost. Search your memories to find out where you lost your love for your purpose. Was it at your job that you clocked into every day when you preferred to operate your business? Maybe you lost it because running your business has depleted your funds and you have yet to see a profit, so now you're just over it.

Wherever you have lost it, start back tracking the steps of your journey so that you can recapture the love you've lost. It is in the recapturing of your first love, that you will find your passion. As my pastor often says, you prosper when you pursue with passion.

Journal Entry #30

I sat in a classroom full of adolescent children, and realized that I was simply struggling and unhappy with my present state of being. The classroom seemed to be a jail that I was locked in with short, sticky cellmates keeping me company.

I was miserable. I had attempted to understand what was going on with me, but I continued to come up empty. I was clearly mistaken to think that this day to day living was all that there was for me. Why had I settled into my job and gotten comfortable with just living? Where was my drive–where did the love go?

There was no drive in me to strive towards anything. My branding and marketing firm, Kreative Kulture was up and in full operation. What more was there to do? The company was helping businesses everywhere expand their reach, revenue, and relevance on a weekly basis. Isn't that success–was I not done with this business? Complacency had taken a seat on me, and it was more evident than ever before.

I had to shake it off. I had to believe that there was more to me than what I was currently experiencing. I was a 'boss' with deep water potential. I knew that God had purposed me to produce, and had graced me to always abound. There was no way I could just stop there. I had to go from faith to faith and glory to glory. Something had to give, and I knew exactly what it was going to be—mundane living.

My passion had to be reignited for the work God had given me to complete. Kreative Kulture was one of the biggest movements that I had produced thus far, but I couldn't stop there. Coming to work every day was me simply enduring a life that I was meant to enjoy.

From one 'boss' to another, choose today to strive towards thriving. You are a 'boss', that has been called to live an abundant life. If you have found that through the journey, you are passionless or lacking passion, I admonish you to go back to the drawing board. You were produced with a purpose on purpose, remember? You must remember the why, so you can continue to do what—you do.

Epilogue

Now, I know that most bosses have certain commonalities, so I am sure that some of you have read ahead, as oppose to taking this one day at a time. So now, I encourage you to go back to the beginning—digest each entry, and take note of the introspection that each day requires. The goal here is to ensure that you put in the work, and not just become familiar with the work that must be done. Remember that the elevator to success is broken, but there are stairs. Do not flake out—go be great! Be bold. Be brave. Be 'bossy'!